HOW TO GROW YOUR ONLINE BUSINESS

CONTENTS

INTRODUCTION

Growing an online business requires careful planning and strategic execution. In today's digital age, where competition is erce, it is crucial to employ executive strategies to stand out and attract customers. This guide aims to provide valuable insights and practical tips on how to grow your online business. We will explore various aspects such as optimizing your website for search engines, leveraging social media platforms, creating compelling content, building a strong brand identity, nurturing customer relationships, and exploring new marketing channels. By implementing these proven methods, you can enhance your online presence, expand your customer base, and ultimately drive sustainable growth for your business.

Step One
Setting the Foundation for Success in Your Online Business

Creating a strong foundation is crucial for the success of your online business. This step involves setting clear goals, identifying your target audience, and establishing a solid brand identity. Let's delve into each aspect:

Plan Your Goals: Start by planning your business objectives. What do you want to achieve? Are you aiming to increase sales, expand your customer base, or enhance brand awareness? Setting specific, measurable, achievable, relevant, and time-bound (SMART) goals will , services, and marketing e orts. Conduct market research to identify their demographics, preferences, and pain points. This information will help you create targeted marketing campaigns that resonate with your ideal customers.

Build a Strong Brand Identity: Develop a compelling brand identity that distinguishes your business from competitors. This includes designing a memorable logo, selecting a color palette, de ning your brand voice, and creating a consistent visual style across all online platforms.

Establish a Professional Website: Your website serves as the virtual storefront for your online business. Ensure it is user-friendly, visually appealing, and optimized for search engines. Make sure your website features high-quality content, easy navigation, clear call-to-actions, and secure payment options.

Develop a Content Strategy: Content is king in the online realm. Create a content strategy that focuses on providing valuable and engaging content to your target audience. This can include blog posts, videos, infographics, or podcasts. Consistently publishing relevant content will attract and retain your audience, boost your search engine rankings, and position you as an industry expert.

By following these foundational steps, you will lay a solid groundwork for your online business growth. In the subsequent steps, we will explore executive marketing strategies, customer engagement techniques, and ways to expand your reach in the digital landscape.

Step two
Building an E ective Online Marketing Strategy

In today's digital landscape, having a well-crafted online marketing strategy is vital for the growth and success of your business. This chapter will guide you through the key components of an e ective online marketing strategy that can drive tra c, generate leads, and increase conversions.

UnderstandingYourTargetAudience: Start by delving deeper into your target audience's needs, preferences, and online behavior. This knowledge will allow you to tailor your marketing e orts to e ectively reach and engage with your potential customers.

Search Engine Optimization (SEO): Enhance your website's visibility on search engines by implementing SEO techniques. Optimize your website's content, meta tags, and URLs, conduct keyword research, and build high-quality backlinks. This will help improve your organic search rankings and drive organic trace to your website.

Pay-Per-Click Advertising (PPC): Consider implementing PPC advertising campaigns, such as Google AdWords or social media ads, to target specific keywords or demographics. PPC can provide immediate visibility and drive targeted trace to your website, helping you reach your marketing goals faster.

Social Media Marketing: Leverage the power of social media platforms to connect with your audience, build brand awareness, and foster engagement. Develop a social media strategy, create compelling content, and utilize paid advertising options to expand your reach and drive tra c to your website.

Email Marketing: Build an email list and develop targeted email campaigns to nurture leads and foster customer loyalty. Deliver valuable content, personalized o ers, and exclusive promotions to your subscribers, ensuring that your emails are engaging, mobile-friendly, and comply with relevant regulations.

In uencer Marketing: Collaborate with in uential individuals or brands within your industry to leverage their reach and credibility. Identify relevant in uencers, establish partnerships, and create authentic and impactful content that resonates with their followers.

By incorporating these components into your online marketing strategy, you will be well-positioned to increase your online visibility, attract a larger audience, and ultimately grow your online business. In the following chapters, we will delve into each component in greater detail, providing practical tips and insights to help you implement a successful marketing strategy.

Step three

Maximizing Website Performance and User Experience

we will focus on optimizing your website's performance and user experience to ensure a seamless and engaging online journey for your visitors. A well-designed and user-friendly website can significantly impact your business's success by improving conversions, reducing bounce rates, and increasing customer satisfaction.

Responsive Web Design: With the growing use of mobile devices, it is crucial to have a responsive website that adapts to di erent screen sizes. Ensure your website is mobile-friendly, loads quickly, and use a seamless browsing experience across various devices.

User-Friendly Navigation: Design intuitive navigation menus and clear site architecture to help visitors easily nd the information they need. Implement a search bar, use descriptive labels for navigation buttons, and minimize the number of clicks required to access key pages.

Compelling Visual Design: Create a visually appealing website that aligns with your brand identity. Use high-quality images, appropriate color schemes, and visually pleasing layouts to capture visitors' attention and leave a lasting impression.

Streamlined Checkout Process: If you have an ecommerce business, optimize your checkout process to minimize cart abandonment. Simplify the steps, provide multiple payment options, or guest checkout, and instill trust through secure payment gateways.

Website Speed and Performance: Improve website loading speed by optimizing image sizes, enabling browser caching, and leveraging content delivery networks (CDNs). Monitor your website's performance regularly and address any issues promptly.

A/B Testing and Conversion Optimization: Implement A/B testing to experiment with di erent website elements and determine which versions yield higher conversion rates. Test variations of headlines, call-to-action buttons, forms, and other critical elements to optimize your website's performance.

By focusing on website performance and user experience, you can create a positive online environment that encourages visitors to engage with your content, explore your o erings, and ultimately convert into customers.

we will delve into specific strategies to enhance each aspect of website performance and user experience, providing actionable tips and best practices.

Step four
Content Creation and Marketing for Online Success

We will explore the importance of content creation and marketing in growing your online business. Compelling and valuable content not only attracts and engages your target audience but also establishes your brand as a trusted authority in your industry.

Developing a Content Strategy: Start by planningning your content goals and identifying the topics and formats that resonate with your target audience. Plan a content calendar to ensure consistent delivery of high-quality content that aligns with your business objectives.

Crafting Engaging Content: Create content that captivates your audience and provides them with valuable insights or solutions to their problems. Utilize various formats such as blog posts, videos, infographics, podcasts, or eBooks to cater to different preferences and enhance engagement.

Search Engine Optimization (SEO) for Content: Optimize your content with relevant keywords, meta tags, and headers to improve its visibility on search engines. Conduct keyword research to identify the terms your audience uses and incorporate them naturally into your content.

Guest Blogging and Content Partnerships: Collaborate with industry influencers or authoritative websites by guest blogging or forming content partnerships. This allows you to tap into their existing audience, build credibility, and expand your reach.

Social Media Content Promotion: Share your content across social media platforms to amplify its reach. Tailor your content for each platform, engage with your audience, and leverage social media advertising to target specific demographics and boost visibility.

User-Generated Content: Encourage your audience to generate content related to your brand, such as reviews, testimonials, or social media posts.

User-generated content not only provides social proof but also fosters a sense of community and authenticity around your brand.

By focusing on content creation and marketing, you can establish a strong online presence, attract organic traffic, and cultivate a loyal audience. In the following steps, we will delve into each aspect of content creation and marketing in greater detail, providing actionable strategies and best practices to help you excel in this area.

Step Five
Leveraging Social Media for Business Growth

In this chapter, we will delve into the power of social media and how it can be leveraged to drive business growth. With billions of users actively engaging on various platforms, social media provides an invaluable opportunity to connect with your target audience, build brand awareness, and foster customer loyalty.

Choosing the Right Platforms: Identify the social media platforms that align with your target audience and business objectives. Popular platforms include Facebook, Instagram, Twitter, LinkedIn, YouTube, and Pinterest. Each platform has its own unique characteristics and audience demographics, so choose wisely.

Building a Strong Social Media Presence: Develop a consistent brand voice and visual identity across your social media platforms. Optimize your platform with relevant keywords and compelling descriptions. Regularly update your pro les with fresh content and engage with your audience through comments, likes, and shares.

Content Creation and Curation: Create engaging and shareable content tailored for each platform. Experiment with di erent formats, such as images, videos, live streams, stories, or polls, to diversify your content strategy. Curate relevant content from industry in uencers or thought leaders to provide additional value to your audience.

Social Media Advertising: Utilize paid social media advertising to reach a wider audience and drive targeted traffic to your website. Set clear objectives, and your target audience, and optimize your ad campaigns based on data and insights.

Community Engagement: Foster a sense of community by actively engaging with your audience. Respond to comments, messages, and reviews promptly. Encourage user-generated content and run social media contests or giveaways to encourage participation.

Social Listening and Analytics: Monitor social media conversations and track key metrics using social listening tools and analytics platforms. Gain insights into your audience's preferences, sentiment, and engagement levels, and use this data to re ne your social media strategy.

By e ectively leveraging social media, you can build brand authority, foster meaningful connections with your audience, and drive traffic and conversions for your online business. In the subsequent chapters, we will explore speci c tactics and techniques for each social media platform, providing practical tips and examples to help you succeed in your social media endeavors.

Step six
Expanding Your Reach with Influencer Marketing

In this step, we will delve into the powerful realm of in uencer marketing and how it can amplify your online business growth. Influencer marketing involves collaborating with in uential individuals or brands within your industry to leverage their reach, credibility, and engaged audience.

Identifying Relevant Influencers: Research and identify influencers who align with your target audience and brand values. Consider factors such as their niche, engagement rates, authenticity, and relevance to your industry. Tools like social media listening platforms and influencer marketing platforms can assist in finding suitable influencers.

Building Authentic Relationships: Reach out to influencers with personalized and genuine messages expressing your interest in collaborating. Engage with their content, comment, and share their posts to establish a connection before approaching them for partnership opportunities.

Creating Compelling Influencer Campaigns: Collaborate with influencers to develop impactful campaigns that align with your business goals. Note clear objectives, provide detailed guidelines, and establish metrics to measure the success of the campaign. Allow in uencers creative freedom to ensure authenticity and resonate with their audience.

Leveraging Different Content Formats: Explore various content formats with influencers, such as sponsored posts, reviews, giveaways, or social media takeovers. Encourage influencers to create engaging content that showcases your products or services in an authentic and compelling manner.

Tracking and Analyzing Campaign Performance: Monitor and analyze key performance indicators (KPIs) of your influencer campaigns. Track metrics like engagement rates, reach, website traffic, and conversions. Use this data to assess the effectiveness of your campaigns and make informed decisions for future collaborations.

Building Long-term Partnerships: Foster long-term relationships with influencers who consistently deliver positive results. Nurture these partnerships by providing ongoing support, exclusive offers, and mutual promotion, creating a win-win situation for both parties.

Influencer marketing can significantly expand your brand's reach, increase brand awareness, and drive conversions. In the subsequent steps, we will dive deeper into influencer selection, campaign execution, and measurement techniques, providing practical strategies and examples to help you maximize the benefits of influencer marketing for your online business.

Step Seven
Harnessing the Power of Email Marketing

We will explore the powerful tool of email marketing and how it can drive engagement, nurture customer relationships, and boost conversions for your online business. Email marketing allows you to reach your audience directly, delivering personalized messages and targeted offers.

Building an Email List: Start by building a quality email list of individuals who have willingly opted in to receive communications from your business. Offer valuable incentives such as exclusive content, discounts, or freebies to encourage sign-ups.

Segmenting Your Audience: Divide your email list into segments based on factors like demographics, purchase history, or engagement levels. This enables you to send highly targeted and relevant messages to each segment, maximizing their impact.

Personalizing Email Campaigns: Use customer data to personalize your email campaigns. Address recipients by name, tailor content to their interests, and leverage automation to send triggered emails based on specific actions or events.

Crafting Compelling Email Content: Create engaging and valuable content that resonates with your audience. This can include product updates, educational content, industry insights, or special promotions. Use persuasive copywriting and visually appealing designs to capture attention.

A/B Testing and Optimization: Experiment with di erent elements of your email campaigns, such as subject lines, call-to-action buttons, or send times, through A/B testing. Analyze the results and optimize your campaigns based on data-driven insights.

Nurturing Customer Relationships: Use email marketing to nurture relationships with your customers. Send personalized thank-you emails, request feedback or reviews, and provide post-purchase support. This fosters loyalty and encourages repeat business.

Analyzing Email Metrics: Track email metrics such as open rates, click-through rates, conversions, and unsubscribe rates. Analyzing these metrics allows you to gauge the success of your email campaigns and make data-backed improvements.

Email marketing remains a highly effective strategy for engaging with your audience and driving business growth.

CONCLUSION

Growing an online business requires a holistic approach that encompasses various key strategies. By setting clear goals, understanding your target audience, and establishing a strong brand identity, you lay a solid foundation for success. Optimizing your website, creating compelling content, leveraging social media, harnessing the power of influencers, and utilizing email marketing all contribute to expanding your online presence, attracting customers, and driving conversions. It is crucial to regularly analyze data, adapt your strategies, and stay updated with industry trends. With dedication, perseverance, and the implementation of these proven techniques, you can propel your online business towards sustainable growth and long-term success.

www.ingramcontent.com/pod-product-compliance
Lightning Source LLC
Chambersburg PA
CBHW070855220526
45466CB00005B/2008